Presented to:

_____

From:

_____

Date:

_____

His Only New Command

"A new command I give you:
Love one another.
As I have loved you, so you must love one another.
By this, all men will know that you are my disciples,
if you love one another"
John 13:34

Agnes
Thanks for the umbrella!
God bless!
Allen Autry

Allen Autry

Miracle in a Small Mountain Town

A Collection Of Inspirational Verse

Copyright © 2001 by Allen Autry of text and illustrations
Published by:
Copperfield Publications, Inc.
2601 East Oakland Park Boulevard, Suite 401
Fort Lauderdale, Florida 33306

Illustrations by contemporary American artist,
James F. Williams

Art direction design and production by
Christine Spencer-Bates

Scripture taken from the HOLY BIBLE NEW INTERNATIONAL
VERSION Copyright 1973, 1978, 1984 International Bible Society.
Used by permission of Zondervan Bible Publishers.

First edition

Library of Congress Catalog Number:2001126821
ISBN: 0-9711819-0-X
Printed in Korea

For my wife, Dee,
with love

Contents

Introduction

It is with a tremendous amount of personal joy that I pen these words of introduction to Allen Autry's new offering of poetic praise. One who is enthralled by his writings quickly discovers that he writes not simply from his hand, nor from his head, but especially from his heart.

Allen Autry's life is a testimony to what is read on these pages. One of the first times I remember meeting with him was when he learned he had a brain tumor. The Lord brought him right up to the portal of the valley of the shadow and then put his wonderful hand of healing, blessing, and recovery upon him. I do not believe Allen has ever gotten away from that experience and the value of the gift of life. Every day is truly a gift, and the poems you read on these pages are laced with words of thanksgiving and praise.

My personal prayer is that all who read these words will be drawn closer to the heart of God for passing this way. Thank you, Allen, for sharing your gifts with all of us. You are loved and appreciated.

O.S. Hawkins
President
Annuity Board
Southern Baptist Convention

Dr. O. S. Hawkins has spent thirty years in the ministry. Before his current position, he served as the pastor of First Baptist Church of Dallas, Texas and First Baptist Church of Fort Lauderdale, Florida.

He has authored a dozen religious and inspirational books, including: **Jonah: Meeting the God of Second Chance** and **In Sheep's Clothing.**

Dr. Hawkins' books may be ordered from Amazon.com as well as local bookstores.

Acknowledgments

This collection of verse was inspired from occurrences in the spiritual life of myself and others. This world which God has created for us is most often filled with the conflicting emotions of both sorrow and joy. Many times, events in our lives seem like a two sided coin mirroring both of these two emotions. God's spirit within us makes the heartaches bearable and the joys intense.

The Author's Notes adjoining some of the poems give the genesis for the particular work.

The illustrations by well known Michigan artist James F. Williams were created over long periods of collaboration between the two of us as to exactly how the emotions of the poem could be interpreted by Jim's artistic renderings. Thanks to Jim for his patience with my numerous requests for changes in concepts. Signed graphics from Jim's original oils may be purchased by themselves or together with signed copies of the poems they represent. Both are suitable for framing.

Some of the poems have been submitted and accepted for publication prior to the publishing of this book. But the majority are new works, not published previously. Publication credits are included at the end of the book. Especially thanks to Father Peter Coughlin, Publisher and Christine LaBrass, Editor of *The Bread of Life* Magazine.

My thanks to my musically gifted son, Allen Jr., and my two brothers, Mike and Jerry who acted as a family focus group for these poems.

Thanks to my wife, Dee, a former English teacher, who spent hours reviewing and editing my work.

Thanks to my friends who encouraged me to have these works published in a book.

Thanks to Clive and Christine Bates of Copperfield Publishing for their very personal interest in helping this book to do its very best!

A *Miracle in a Small Mountain Town*

'Twas spring time on the Blue Ridge
and the Jaybird trilled its song.
The wildflowers awoke from slumber
as the days were waxing long.
Yet, in the household was no joy,
for Papa's taken ill.
The doctors sighed, "no hope"
and the preacher mused, "God's will".

Critical care and in a coma
from which they said, "there's no reprieve"
aged four score, affliction seized him
through his life-force it did weave.
Came the children and grandchildren
and his wife around his bed
to bid good-byes and view the last
of this man they dearly loved.

But like the mustard seed of faith,
from that book of old
"Jesus save him", begged the daughter,
to her family, "Pray, be bold".
Dear God, we love him so.
Do not take our daddy yet.
For to you shall be the glory.
And with that pledge, they wept."

God saw their tears and felt their pain.
Their faith moved his mighty hand.
Swiftly, an angel He dispatched
to save a dying man.
Suddenly, Papa's eyes did open
and he gazed up to our faces.
"Where're my shoes?" he fairly shouted.
Then, we knew we'd seen God's graces.

From that hospital dorm he fled
and returned home for quite a while.
The doctors were astounded.
For that, God must have had a smile.
Papa knew he'd bought some time
for his family and God's glory.
He often spoke of Jesus' love
as he fondly told his story.

He'd say, "Jesus is so kind
to let me come home once again,
to embrace my wife and children
and to greet my dear old friends"
In the sun, he walked old pathways
and for many months did live.
Friends said, "He had a way about him
that only God could give."

Papa knew this gift was brief,
a missive from God's heart.
He feared not the life to come
when from this world he must depart.
His last night, we well remember
for he saw Christ slip into his room.
"I'm ready, don't weep" he whispered,
"Jesus has come to take me home."

Friends, this story is not over.
For now Papa lives where angels sing
where the wildflowers bloom forever
and our savior reigns as king
where the Jaybird trills his song
and Springtime never ends
in that land for us God promised
from whence miracles begin.

John 14:2 *"In my father's house are many rooms; if it were not so,
I would have told you. I am going there to prepare a place for you..."*

Miracle in a Small Mountain Town

The father of my wife, when he was in his eighties, was operated on for an aneurysm of the brain. While the doctors were preparing for the operation and doing blood tests it was discovered that he was in the latter stages of deadly leukemia. After the operation, the doctors related that although the operation was successful, that he would die in a few days. He was administered morphine and kept unconsious to make his end easier.

However, my wife and others of the family were concerned that he had never had an opportunity to make his own decision. The family prayed and told the nurses to stop administering morphine. He awoke shortly and demanded to be taken home.

I remember praying with him and how the tears came to his eyes as he praised Jesus for letting him go home again to see his family. His leukemia went into remission for months and the doctors were amazed. His doctor was preparing to write an article on his remission for the medical journal when the sickness returned.

This man was an inspiration to his family and others for the next few months. He told of his love for Jesus often and on the night he died several months later, he told all around him who were in his bedroom that he saw Jesus and other spiritual beings in his room. He told us that he wanted to go with Jesus. During the night, he stretched his arms upward to go with them and shortly he joined his savior in Paradise.

Illustration: "Village in the Valley" Created for this poem by artist, James F. Williams.

A Rose Without a Thorn

From the garden of my heart, yields a rose without a thorn.
A dewdrop on its petal, hails the sun in early morn.
A thing of beauty, quite exquisite, like no other ever seen.
It blooms in all the seasons, scorching drought or April rain.

It inspires me, it delights me
this rose without a thorn.
Its aroma lifts my spirit
to the place our love was born.

By God's own hand, the seed was sown, no credit dare I take.
One morning it appeared, when my heart was set to break.
Yesterday, the barren ground, then astonished, I beheld
a blossom had emerged, where once weeds had overwhelmed.

Today,
treasured memories fondly beckon
to a heart once enchanted by a rose.
God entwined our souls forever
with His love the strand that holds.

Ecc. 4:12 "A cord of three strands is not easily broken"

A Rose Without a Thorn

*This is my intimate feeling in regard to God's hand in the choice of
my wonderful wife and soul mate. We are best friends and confidants.
Truly God is the third strand in the rope of husband and wife relationships.
When that heavenly strand is not present, we witness the heartaches
of failed dreams, broken relationships and children suffering from the
lack of a caring nurturing parentship which God intended. A marriage
blessed by heaven is surely one of our greatest gifts on earth.*

*A*n Old Sea Captain's Prayer

I'm aching and weary and hard of hearing
81 years old and losing my bearing.
A sea captain I was, when I was younger
Good sea legs and my back was stronger,
Mind too.

*I*n that day, the sun polished the sea.
Swooping gulls screeched their shrill melody.
Life to be lived, salt spray in my hair
Clear sailing, nary a cloud anywhere,
Just sky blue.

I beheld giant turtles and whales.
And on occasion, told a few tall tales
To young sons who loved to hear
On return to port, of dad's doin'dare,
My compass true.

*Y*es, all of that, precious memories
Scary talk now, bypass and surgeries.
Is the voyage over, I don't know.
Navigation is harder though.
Must trust You.

I know that my ship is slower.
Lord, guess I lost some power
From all those miles.
Would you take the rudder for a while?
Much obliged to You.

~

We will always love and miss you Dad

Math 12:28   "Come to me, all of you who are weary and
burdened and I will give you rest..."

An Old Sea Captain's Prayer

This poem represents an intensely personal and emotional time in my life and in the life of my two brothers and of course, my mother. My elderly father, a sea captain, had come to the city where I lived to have open heart surgery performed. He wanted to have his children close by during recuperation. During the couple of days, prior to surgery, we spent a lot of intimate hours together. The surgery was successful, but unfortunately, he suffered a delibitating stroke a few days later while recuperating in my home.

The subsequent paralysis and lack of speech was hell on earth which a man of his previously active lifestyle found incredibly tormenting. I would sit by his bedside and show him pictures from his coastal hometown. However, I think that these recollections may have exacerbated his depression.

Dad lived a few months longer. He believed that he was not recovering and he refused to continue eating. He was an exceptionally moral and kind man who believed in God, although he was somewhat shy and not a regular "churchgoer". We, his surviving family, have no doubt that God steered him safely to his final destination.

Me and Jesus

As was often his habit,
The old man sat on the worn bench
near the ancient oak tree
behind the ivy covered old red brick church
which he had attended since a child.

On the late Summer day, he fondly
watched the young children on recess
at Vacation Bible School as they played
near him on the green velvet church yard.

And when they sang "Jesus loves me,
this I know",
the old man's lips moved
and he tapped his foot.

At break, the children swilled the
chilled lemonade and munched their cookies.
When finished, they ran and dove into
a huge pile of leaves under the big old oak tree
next to the elderly witness.
Full of energy and joy, they pushed each other
and rolled around in the leaves
laughing and shrieking.

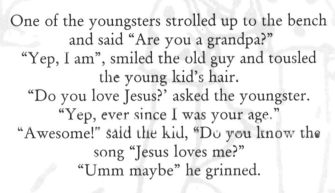

One of the youngsters strolled up to the bench
and said "Are you a grandpa?"
"Yep, I am", smiled the old guy and tousled
the young kid's hair.
"Do you love Jesus?' asked the youngster.
"Yep, ever since I was your age."
"Awesome!" said the kid, "Do you know the
song "Jesus loves me?"
"Umm maybe" he grinned.

The kid waved goodbye as he shouted,
"Well, Me and Jesus got to
hit the leaves now".
Then, he scrambled back into the pile of leaves
with his small friends.
The break ended and the teachers and
their charges returned into the old church.

Furtively, the old man glanced around the
grounds.
Slowly, he eased his arthritic frame from the
bench.
Carefully, he ambled over to the pile of leaves,
while leaning on his cane.
For a few moments, he gazed intently at the
pile of leaves.
Once more, he cautiously turned his stooped
torso to see if anyone were watching.
Seeing no one, he smiled, removed his old cap
from his white maned head and uttered,
"Well, Me and Jesus got to hit the leaves now."

Suddenly, he threw himself with abandon into
the pile of leaves and grass.
Seemingly for good measure,
and while grinning from ear to ear,
he rolled around two or three times
in the crackling leaves.

Out of breath, but still smiling, he rested
on his back a few minutes.
The old gentleman eased himself to his feet,
put on his cap and tidily brushed himself off

Slightly limping, he sauntered towards home
down the shaded sidewalk.
"Do I know 'Jesus Loves Me' ", he muttered
with an impish look on his face.
And if you were close enough, you might have
heard him softly singing as he bobbed his head
along the way.

"Jesus loves me, this I know,
for the Bible tells me so.
Little ones to him belong,
We are weak, but he is strong
Yes, Jesus loves me
Yes, Jesus loves me
Yes, Jesus loves me
The Bible tells me so."

*"Train a child in the way he should go, and when he is old
he will not turn from it." Proverbs 22:6*

Me and Jesus

*So many of us have fond memories of how we received the sweet
message of the Lord Jesus. The exuberance we feel from his love
does not decrease with age, but increases, as we reflect on the many
times we called on Jesus and he answered us. The old man in this
piece is but another happy child of Jesus, grown older perhaps,
but still gleefully acknowledging the lordship of Jesus in his life.*

*E*piphany in a Taxi

She danced and she whirled
to the calls and the propositions
under the blistering lights
of the back street cabaret
naked as the day that she was born
her mama's baby girl on that July morn
nineteen years ago.

Tonight she is barely able
to gyrate on the table
and maintain her cocaine smile
for the patrons at the show.

Finally at 4 AM,
legislated immorality abates.
She leaves her dressing room, perspiring,
in leotards and a mini skirt.
Overwhelmed by despair
with muddled thinking,
she hails a cab on the deserted city street.

Then, in the warm solitaire
of her backseat metered sanctuary,
she closes her eyes.
She tries to remember how it all began.
When did she trade her tortured life
for this final abyss?
From whence came this pathos of dread
that darkens her soul?
Ah, how did it all go wrong?

Then softly, to her ear
sounds come as in a prayer.
In the mirror,
she sees the familiar face of the young driver.
His lips are quietly moving.

In irritation, she snaps,
"Did you speak to me?
Are you praying?
Who are you?"

Then, he smiles at her
from the mercuried glass reflection
and softly declares,
"I have driven you nightly
and I have seen you hold tightly
to a dream of a life away from this."

"Tonight there is no charge for the fare
and yes, it was a prayer
for you."

"Relax, while I drive
and let me tell you of another life
that awaits for you."

"Jesus sees your distress and feels your pain.
He waits but for you to call his name.
Then, He will close that door
which you in sin, opened so long ago."

"His forgiveness and his love and his strength
will be yours,
as will that great peace for which you yearn."

There was stillness in the cab
as she considered
the strange words which she had just heard.

Then, a sudden stirring bolted her heart,
as her soul was electrified by Cosmic Love.
Tears of joy flooded, unbidden, into her eyes.

"Yes", she uttered as she wept
and at that moment in eternity,
Jesus Christ filled her life,
in a taxi,
at dawn.

*Eph. 2:8 "For it is by grace you have been saved through
faith and this not from yourselves, it is the gift of God."*

Epiphany in a Taxi

*This piece was inspired by a woman that I knew,
who had led a promiscuous life. But due to God's graces, she had changed
into a strong and spiritual citizen of the community. When we call his
name, Christ can meet us anywhere and at any time, whether in a castle or
the back seat of a beat up taxi.*

*U*nexpected Encounter in Edinburgh

The mighty and aged castle of Edinburgh
earlier had cast its long shadow
on the historic city street of Scotland's capitol.
But now the late October afternoon had turned dark
and wet as the drizzle turned into driving rain.

The native Scots
and the visitors to the highland country
scampered to their destinations in the city.

On vacation, I with head tucked down,
chuckling at my sudden predicament,
hurried to meet my wife at our hotel.
Trying, without success, to avoid the cold rain,
as I scampered along the slippery walkway.

Then, unexpectedly,
I saw her.
She was a wee lassie of a girl,
not yet a woman,
sitting on the wet cold sidewalk
of the busy street.
She was slumped against the gray stone wall
of a merchant shop.
Her long blond tresses were
drenched and matted by the chilling rain.
Her head was bowed.

She avoided eye contact with the bristling throng.
No professional hustler here,
someone's daughter.
She might have been pretty at another time.
Now, shivering,
Misery personified.

She had a blanket pulled around her legs.
Her soaked shivering dog huddled close to her side
as the frigid wind raked the two of them.
She shared part of her blanket
to cover the back of her faithful canine comrade.

By her side at the edge of the blanket
was a small pot for collections
which did not come.

She held a scrawled sign,
now smeared from the rain,
KOSOVO WAR REFUGEE

In curiosity, I stopped a few paces later
under cover of an awning.
I observed her from my sheltered vantage.
Astonished, I watched
as the streaming hundreds of sidewalk pilgrims passed
by her.

They gave not a glance her way
nor tossed a shilling to the pitiful waif.

Troubled, I walked back and stood facing her.
"God bless you.", I uttered,
which somehow sounded hollow and inadequate.
I clinked some British pounds into her canister.
Conned or not, chicanery or truth, it didn't matter.
I had to make this minimal effort
to salve my own conscience.

She slowly raised her head
and glanced up at me through the pouring rain.
Her eyes were of the palest blue,
I have ever seen,
eyes with no hope.

She briefly nodded her head
to acknowledge my penance.
Then, she seemed embarrassed
and looked away.

No smile of gratitude came from her.
Did I expect one?
With a feeling of emptiness,
in silence, I turned and walked away.

A half block later,
I paused to look back over my shoulder.
She was gone.

I knew that I should have done more.
I felt inept and ashamed.
I prayed that God send some Samaritan
more courageous than I, to her aid.

1 John 3:18 "Dear friends, let us not love with words or tongue
but with actions and in truth."

Encounter in Edinburgh

On a trip to Scotland one late October, I was walking down the
street in Edinburgh, just after the end of the war in Kosovo. Many
victims of this war had fled to Britain. As I was rushing through
the rain, I saw a young woman and her dog sprawled against
the side of a store front. She held a sign identifying herself
as a victim of that war. She was ignored by the passersby.
The story pretty well speaks for itself. That scene will
always be etched in my memory.

*W*hose Babies are These?

*W*hose babies are these that squirm
in the warmth and the dark of their mothers bellies?
A being in process,
Loved and watched by the angels, gently soothing
Not yet given over to us, but soon
Adored by heaven, divine creations.
Whose babies are these?

*S*o quiet, no one can hear them, nor see them
Yet inside there is a spark
A porcelain hand moves, a tiny leg trembles
A little face wrinkles, a wisp of thumb meets lip
There is no sound, but that of a heartbeat
Whose babies are these?

I am has breathed life into these who will be
Who shall He trust with His gift
Who will speak for this defenseless creation of His love
Who will be given over this charge from the angels
Whose babies are these?

*Math.25:40 "I tell you the truth, whatever you did for these the least of these
brothers of mine, you did for me."*

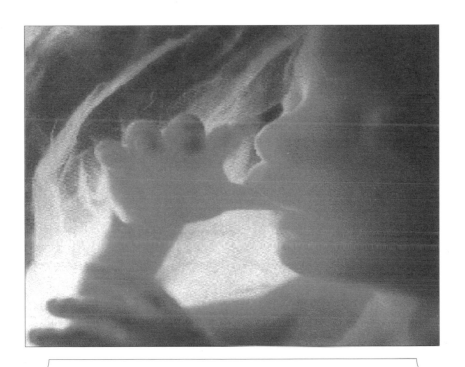

Whose Babies are These?

The bible is wrought with illustrations of the fact that God recognized the unborn as a human being. Certainly, one of the greatest illustrations is that he told certain characters in the Bible, who the child was that Mary carried in her womb.

This verse is dedicated to the volunteers and staff at The Hope Pregnancy Centers as they faithfully and lovingly assist young mothers-to-be while telling them of God's love for their unborn child.

A Nest for The Killing Bird

In the night, as sleep evades me, I recall when once I flew
As an eagle into combat when the smell of death was new.
A southern country boy who'll never be the same
Shiny wings upon my shoulders, off to live my dream.

The Forrestal was my nest and I became a Killing Bird.
Young pilots soiled their trousers as the aircraft guns we
heard.
No mission did we question as the orders passed each day.
God, just let us live, we'd pray then soar away.

Hellfire and destruction, I rained on land and sea
Vaporizing faceless hundreds, uncountable by me.
Targets they were called, yet to myself I asked
God's children aren't we all, while feigning stoic in my task.

Mission after Mission, from the carrier we'd repeat
Then, my friend and navigator perished in his seat.
Sorrow etched that day, in tears I limped back to the nest
That night, I wrote a letter, told his mom he was the best.

Years can't staunch the pain from that tour I spent in 'Nam
Innocence buried in a paddy, am I forever damned?
In your nest Lord, is there room for a Killing Bird like me?
"Yes, but son, you are now a dove. Faith has set you free."

*I Peter 1:3 "In his great mercy, He has given us new birth into
a living hope through the resurrection of Jesus Christ from the
dead and into an inheritance that can never perish"*

A Nest for The Killing Bird

*This is the story of a contemporary of mine, hero of the
Vietnam War, as told to me one day by him as we
were sharing lunch. As he related his wartime experience,
there was anguish mixed with pride regarding the
service he had given for his country. He was devoted
to his duty, but due to the many lives he had
taken in battle, he expressed doubt as to the
compassion of God in offering forgiveness.*

*Illustration: "A Nest for The Killing Bird" Created
for this poem by artist, James F. Williams.*

*A*be's Prayer

Lord, disaster has fallen like a plague upon this great land.
The Union is torn asunder.
Awake in the darkness of night, I can neither rest nor slumber.
My whole body shakes from the dread of misdeed.
I can not ebb the flow of sweat which soaks my bed.
What evil have I wrought upon this nation conceived by You?

I fear to close my eyes,
for the wounded and the dying cry out to me.
No food will I consume,
for I smell the cannon and I feel the heat of battle.
My mind reels as brothers shed the blood of brothers.
Due to my steadfastness,
thousands shall perish in the blossom of their youth.
My eyes are like dust and I can weep no more.
Lord, I feel so alone and I am filled with such despair

My mind is no longer clear.
All is seen through a mist of blood.
I am uncertain of the truth of my actions.
Yet, did you not affirm to my soul that
"All men are created equal."

Lord, I beg for the wisdom, strength and peace
which you promise to those who love you and obey you.
It is your wings which must lift me
to finish the labor begun by your spirit.
I am an empty vessel which longs
to be filled by your love and your power.
Lord, be with your servant now
in the moment of his greatest need.

Amen

"For God did not give us a spirit of timidity, but a spirit of power and of love and of self-discipline." 2 Tim 1:7

Abe's Prayer

What a tumultuous time in our nation's history! I am not a civil war buff.
But, often I have thought about the loneliness of Lincoln's life during that
period. Both sides were angry at him for the loss and destruction caused by
the war. He was said to be a spiritual man. This piece illustrates what I
would have imagined his prayer to be based upon his belief and his character.
Historical records indicate that he prayed often during that incredibly
emotional time of his life.

Illustration: "Abe's Prayer" Created for this poem by artist,
James F. Williams.

The Little-Church-by-the-Sea

Two cute kids of six and kind of shy.
Eddy'd glance at Suzie to catch her eye.
At Sunday School, chairs side by side
She'd blush at Eddy and grin real wide.
She slipped in his Bible a note one day.
"Eddy, can we be friends, I hope and pray?"
Two innocent children with sparkling eyes
What will be as the years roll by?
In the Little-Church-by-the Sea

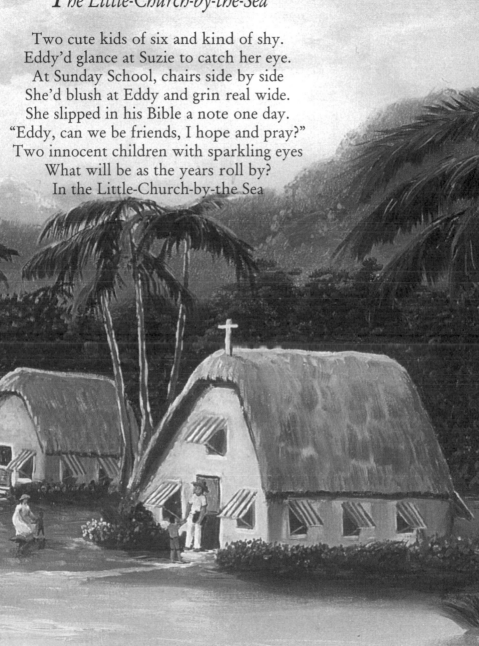

One August Sunday, in their thirteenth year,
Suzie whispered at church in Eddy's ear,
"I feel God's pull at the alter call
Will you walk with me, so I won't fall?"
Eddy uttered "Yes, for I feel it too.
We both love Jesus and his love is true."
Hand in hand they walked down the aisle,
The preacher waited with a loving smile.
In the Little-Church-by-the-Sea

A few years later, on a crisp Fall day,
Eddy declared, "Suzie, I've something to say.
You know I've loved you all my life.
And I have prayed so hard that you'll be my wife.
But before you say what's on your heart,
In my prayer there is another part.
I must leave this place and can not stay,
God's called me to a mission far away
From the Little-Church-by-the-Sea."

Suzie silently turned and bowed her head.
She prayed for wisdom for their life ahead.
Then she kissed his lips and fluffed his hair.
"With you, Eddy my love, I'll go anywhere.
When God has called, we must not hide.
I will be your wife and serve by your side."
In the month of May, the church bells rang
They said their vows as the small choir sang
In the Little-Church-by-the-Sea

Eighteen years of service in a country small,
They taught God's love to one and all.
They raised four children in that foreign land,
A family transplanted to be God's hand.
But often, when the day was done
And the warm winds banished the setting sun
Eddy and Suzie would hold hands and say
"You know I'd like to go back one day
To the Little-Church-by-the-Sea"

The peasants adored them, but alas, one day
The rebels blew the mission away.
Of Suzie and Eddy no trace was found.
In the jungle, some say, in the ground.
Grief was great for they were loved
By children and friends and God above.
In their hometown, two statues were made
Of Eddy and Suzie with this plaque engraved
In front of the Little-Church-by-the-Sea

OUR FRIENDS, EDDY AND SUZIE LOST THEIR LIFE,
SERVING GOD ON EARTH AS MAN AND WIFE.
PART OF THE GREATEST STORY EVER TOLD,
THEY SERVE HIM NOW ON STREETS OF GOLD.

BOTH BLESSED OF GOD AND LOVED OF SON
GLORY TO GOD. HIS WILL BE DONE.

*"You did not choose me, but I choose you and appointed you to go and bear fruit,
fruit that will last...This is my command: Love each other."* John 15:16

The Little Church by the Sea

*There have been many stories of martyred missionaries.
These people have left family and friends to obey God's
call to their lives. They do not think of themselves as
heroic although they surely know of the hardship and
challenges they will face. I read of a couple in South
America who were killed by rebel forces and their bodies
never found. Since the beginning, possible loss of life has
been a risk to these emissaries of our Lord. We can
only thank God for their commitment and the sacrifices
they make while spreading the Gospel throughout the world.*

Lord, Did You Sob with Shoulders Shaking?

Lord, help me understand such love
that gave your son for me.
Did your heart break as the father
of this man from Galillee?

Oh, beloved God eternal,
was there a tear you could not hide
When a Roman blade was thrust
into your son, my Saviour's side?

Did you fling your arm across your eyes,
did you sob with shoulders shaking
when He cried out from the cross,
"My God, hast thou me forsaken?"

The most wrenching pain, I believe you felt,
ever known in earth or heaven
was at the moment of His sacrifice,
when your greatest gift was given.

Matt 27: 46-54 "..Jesus cried out in a loud voice, 'My God, my God why have you forsaken me?'..The earth shook and the rocks split...they were terrified and exclaimed, "Surely, he was the son of God."

Lord, Did You Sob with Shoulders Shaking?

Students of the word know that the Bible states that Jesus felt that God had turned his spirit away from him at his last moment on the cross. At this time, our Saviour carried all the sin of the world, so as to be our atoning sacrifice. The scripture declares that God has emotions including love, anger and sorrow. What sorrow must he have felt during the pain of his only son, Jesus, when Jesus said, "My God, hast thou forsaken me?" Was the deluge of emotion experienced by God manifested in the recorded unusual events surrounding Christ's death? These events included the deceased "saints" arising from their graves, the temple curtain being torn apart and total darkness briefly covered the earth while earthquakes split the hillsides. Were these events the equivalent of the "weeping of Heaven"? I believe so and this time of sorrow by our God was the inspiration for this piece.

Illustration: "Forgiven" created for this poem by artist, James F. Williams.

The View from The Cross

Father, behold Mother Mary kneeling and weeping at my
feet.
She obediently tended me as a child,
not fully understanding my deity.
She is blessed among women.

Now father, dry her tears and preserve her from all harm.
She is my beloved mother on earth
and will be my daughter in heaven.

Father, there is beloved John,
his sweet head bowed in pain and guilt.
He forsook family and friends to follow me.
Father, bind his heart and strengthen his resolve.
He will give all for my sake.
Oh, how I love him.

Father, the centurions gaze up at me.
Some believe but are afraid.
The others will soon behold your awesome powers.
Father, let my death and resurrection melt their doubting
hearts.

Father, the chariot of Pilate rumbles by.
With head averted, he ignores the lamb.
Father, bless his wife, she upheld me against the crowd.
His cowardice as the servant of Satan was preordained.
Father, on your breath, whisper your truth to him.

Father! My eyes no longer see. My ears are grown deaf.
Father! Your spirit has fled from me!
My father, my God, why have You forsaken me?

Father! I love you.
Father! It is done.

Father, You have raised me again to your side
Once more, I bask in your brilliance and your love.
Through my sorrows, mankind may now redeem itself.
Father, You and I again are one.
And now, they may be one with us.

Amen

"And surely I am with you always, to the very end of the age." Mark 28:20

View from the Cross

What must have been Christ's thoughts and prayers on the cross as he did his Father's bidding? Did he look around and make observations? It appears that he did, based upon the scriptures. Due to his spiritual character we may imagine how he was reconciling the actions of the cast of characters while seeking to forgive them.

A Prayer for Restoration

W hen my heart is all aquiver
When darkness seals my world
When evil thoughts engulf me
As Satan's flag unfurls

I flee to sanctuary
to pray and read your book of old
Let your peace descend upon me
Let your spirit balm my soul.

Amen

"I have told you these things so that in me you may have peace" John 16:33

Prayer of Restoration

*Jesus did not promise us that we would not have trials
in this world controlled by Satan. He did promise
us that his great gift to us during these times would
be wisdom and peace. I have found that during
great tribulations in my personal life, which have
included a brain tumor and other events too
unpleasant to recount, that the peace of Jesus is
the one constant.*

*A*rmour of Heaven

Demons of Darkness, scatter before us
for a shield divine safeguards our heart.
Spawns of Satan strain to grasp us
but the sword of Gideon their midst shall part.

Creatures of Hell clamor and shiver
as before the King, they shriek "Retreat!"
Praise Son of God, the armour of heaven
He guides us safe through Hell's defeat.

*"Finally, be strong in the Lord and his mighty power. Put on the full armour
of God, so that you can take your stand against the Devil's schemes. For our
struggle is not against flesh and blood...but against powers of this dark
world..." Ephesians 6:13.*

Armour of Heaven

*In dismay, Paul expressed in the book of Acts, how the Devil wars within us.
Our body is constantly being pulled toward evil actions due to the seduction
of the dark forces around us. It is only due to the spiritual armour obtained
through Christ's sacrifice that we may hold Satan's forces at bay.*

*H*ell's Boulevard

Why do we sin? It's so much fun!
The Devil knows it's true
Hell's Boulevard, so sweetly paved,
to entice me and you.

Yet, God knows great things I long to do,
to prove my love for him.
But drawn each day these mortal feet
to trod Sin Street again.

I can not fathom nor plumb the depth
of my savior's love for me.
Nor do I believe that I will ever be
the man that I ought to be.

I must call that name and call it soon,
that clefts the Devil's spell.
For Christ gave his all upon the tree
to save us all from hell.

*Romans 10:9-10 "...if you confess with your mouth that Jesus is Lord and
believe in your heart that God raised him from the dead, you will be saved.
For it is with your heart that you believe and are justified, and it is with
your mouth that you confess and are saved."*

Hell's Boulevard

*This was inspired by a preacher at the church which my
son attends. I went with my son to this particular service.
The young preacher was unusually candid in his recounting
of his sinful life before he came to Christ. At one point in
his remarks, he said, "Why do we sin? It's so much fun!"
Everyone chuckled, because we all knew how close to the
mark that observation really was. Think about it. Hasn't
the forbidden fruit always been the tastiest?
"The Devil knows it's true."*

*This poem is engraved on a brass plaque which is dedicated
to and hangs within The Mission of St. Francis, a Christian
substance abuse rehabilitation clinic located in
Fort Lauderdale, Florida.*

*T*he Story of Love

"I send..." said God

"I obey..." said Jesus

"I treasure..." said Mary

"I wash..." said Jesus

"I kiss..." said Judas

"I am..." said Jesus

" I condemn..." said Pilate

"I die..." said Jesus

"I doubt..." said Man

"I arose..." said Jesus

"I believe..." said Man

"I forgive..." said Jesus

"I love..." said God

"I send..." 1 John 4:10;   "I obey..." John 10:18;   "I treasure..." Luke 2:19;
"I wash..." John 13:8;   "I kiss..." Matt 26:49;   "I am..." John 18:37;
"I condemn..." Luke 6:25;   "I die..." Luke 24:46;   " I doubt..." Matt 27:41
"I arose..." John 20:20;   "I believe..." John 20:28;   "I forgive..." 1 John 1:9;
"I love..." John 3:16

Story of Love

This little piece is the message of the New Testament told with two words indicative of certain key scriptures. It is a good piece for children to learn so as to simplify the story of the "Good News" it also helps with the memorization of key scriptures. Can you identify the verses? Some of the lyrics may represent more than one Biblical scripture.

*H*oly Spirit, *Tender Teacher*

How ephemeral, how serene
is the nature of the Holy Spirit.
At times, coursing through my consciousness,
like a river lost, but yearning to be found.

Eternal wisdom is the Spirit.
It awaits as Solomon's treasure to be discovered
by the diligent searcher, the true believer.

Yet, a mystery so delicate,
that my sinful thoughts will send it scurrying
as a wide eyed deer
bounding from the glades afire.

Lord, I fall prostrate, once again asking for Your forgiveness
and the Spirit groans and returns to me.
Perhaps it never abandoned me,
but if not, in my sin I could not find it.

Why does it withdraw?
Tender and elusive, it departs me, sorrowed
when wounded by my sin,
a proud guest who does not linger when not wanted.

To me, Lord, you have promised wisdom and peace
when I call your Holy Name
when I entrust your mastery over my soul.
Come to me again, I beg you
Holy Spirit, Teacher Mine.

*Jesus replied... "But the Counselor, the Holy Spirit, whom the father
will send in my name will teach you all things and remind you of
everything that I have said to you" John 14:26*

Holy Spirit, Tender Teacher

*Jesus promised to all believers that we would
have the indwelling of the Holy Spirit. But, as we well
know, the "indwelling" and being "filled with the spirit"
are two different things. We must raise the Spirit by
our prayer life and by our walk with Christ. When, we
sin, the Spirit and its wisdom retreats until once again
we call on the Spirit due to our heartfelt need to have
Jesus as lord in our life.*

*This piece tries to catch the elusiveness of this constant
struggle that the apostle Paul so well described.*

RAGGEDY MAN

A couple stopped their car when the light turned red
near a raggedy man on the road ahead.
A bearded thin face, threadbare old clothes
stooped and shivering with holes in his shoes.
He had nothing to say.

The husband glanced at the bum and smirked.
Laughed at his sign NEED FOOD WILL WORK.
Driving away, she muttered, "He stunk.
Can't waste our money on a dirty old drunk."
And they turned away.
~

Once poor, a man became a millionaire,
Came true, the American dream last year.
We knew him when ends didn't meet.
The good life, now on Easy Street
It's been a good day.

A chalet in Aspen, his little red jag
A tuck here and there keeps 'way the sag
Asked to help poor kids in town
"Can't do it, he said, stock market's down."
And he turned away.

Two businessmen lunch in a small cafe
Pondering a tragedy a world away.
"Ten thousand killed by a storm in Honduras.
People starving and ill, sounds real serious
I hear their homes were blown away."

"Red Cross takes up a collection today.
Let's give a donation. What do you say?
Spend money on foreigners? I don't know why.
People starve in America. Pass the pie."
And they turned away.

～

Why do we flinch from doing our part
To ease the burden on our brothers heart?
Can't we see his tears and feel his pain?
Is pity held hostage to personal gain?
Why do we turn away?

For someday, the Book will be opened wide,
inscribed in blood our name inside.
Then, the saddest words He could ever say.
"Children, I was the heart you broke that day."
Will He turn away?

*1 John 3:17 "If anyone has material possessions and sees his brother
in need and has no pity on him, how can the love of God be in him?"*

Raggedy Man

*There is such conflict within us when we encounter
a person in need who asks us for charity. We are
torn between cynicism and the desire to give.
Often we are afraid that we may be taken
advantage of by the situation. Unfortunately,
due to our cynical nature, we are more apt to err
on the side of caution and not assist the person.
We have all felt this dichotomy of emotion.*

*In one of the verses, I recall having asked a man
whom I had known for a while to contribute to
a local charity. This man had become very wealthy
in the years that I knew him. He told me that he
was not making any contributions, due to the
decline in the stock market. He is worth millions,
but could not give even a small amount for a
worthwhile cause. He told me how so many people
were after him to give. I am sure that this is true.*

*I believe that we should look for reasons to give the
needy and not seek reasons not to give. Even
the gift of a small amount may inspire others
and lift the spirits of those being favored.*

S*tuff*

Oh Lord, I've done it now.

Head over heels in debt again,
with all the stress these credit cards bring.
I just want so much stuff.
I want to be noticed.
Clothes, fancy jewelry, too much car, show-off stuff.

Forgive me Lord,
Stuff brings no joy,
just a temporary anesthesia to ease the pain of you
not in my life.
Once, I knew you.
Fill me again with your Holy Spirit.

I John 1:9. If we confess our sins, he is faithful and will forgive us our sins
and purify us from all unrighteousness.

Stuff
It's a material world. The shine is hard to ignore.
We are tempted toward self-indulgence, while
ignoring the issues of God in our life. Only by a
consistant prayer life can we withstand the temptations
and give the Holy Spirit the invitation to fill our lives.

The Preacher

Once, he had been God's herald to millions,
a dispatcher of The Good News.
He counseled troubled presidents
and was a vanguard of a nation's morality.

He had held the hand of the fearful,
the sick
and the dying.
He was a harbinger of the apocalypse to come.
Thousands said,
"I came to know the Lord through him."

A king's treasure had been in his coffers
to succor the needy.
He brought tears to the driest eyes
with his fervent predications of a better life
through The One.

Truly, he had been Someone.

But, now the preacher has stumbled
and has fallen.
Now his head is bowed in prayer asking for forgiveness.
Now his feet are mired in the sins of lust and acquisition.

Pictures, the media barons have pictures
and have her chronicle of the sordid event.
Yes, for sure, stumbled and fallen
A sinner like the rest of us,
and we are ashamed that we said
that he was Someone.

Yet, thousands found the true path through his entreaties.
Who will thank God for the preacher?
For he turned many away from a life of destruction.

Upon reflection,
perhaps he was Someone.
Maybe more so than most.

The Preacher

*Millions have come to Christ through the public ministries
of imperfect men. The fact that these proud men have
stumbled does not make the Gospel they disbursed any less perfect.*

*If God is to judge us by our works, then certainly, those
ministers who have led so many to Christ, but they
themselves have stumbled in the public view, still will
have many crowns for their work. They, like we all, will
be forgiven for their errors if they truly repent.*

The Redefinment of Love

Saith the Word,
When He breathed as a man,
Only one new command
To his perplexed band
He gave.

And thus, He explained
"Treat your neighbor as self?
Put that rule on the shelf.
For you don't treat yourself
that well."

He said, "Dearest friends,
through joy and tears
You have known me three years.
Does man's self love compare
with mine?"

He said,
"Respect the Big Ten,
As God's laws coding sin.
But no man can win
but through Me.

Thus, heard the twelve,
In a room up above
This redefinment of love
And remembered the dove
upon Him.

"Hearken closely.
This command new,
Love each brother true
As I have loved you,
do this."

For us,
Broken and spilled
At dawn on the hill
He obeyed Father's will
Greatest love.

John 13:34 "A new command I give you, love one another. As I have loved you, so you must love one another. By this, all men will know that you are my disciples, if you love one another"

The Redefinement of Love

*Jesus only gave one new commandment
which was John 13:34. However, with
this new commandment, he changed the
definition of how God's children should
love each other. Prior to this utterance
by Christ, the previous standard of love
had been the Old Testament standard,
"Love your neighbor as you love yourself..."*

*Jesus knew that sometimes we did not love
ourselves very well. Thus our standard of
love for each other is in constant flux according
to our feeling of well being, a very unstable
standard of love. At the end of his
ministry, in John 13:34, Jesus disclosed to his
disciples that he gave us a new commandment:
"Love each other as I have loved you..."
This then was to be the new standard of
our Christian behavior towards each
other-
To love as Jesus loved.*

CARRY ON! CARRY ON!
(Sherlie's Song)

Today, I glance around me at the blessings that surround me
And my griefs, I know, are only worlds that pass.
In a frothing icy sea, which You alone can calm for me,
I struggle to trust the faith that lasts.

Lord, help me to remember, as these storms buff me in December
that your flame of love stills warms me deep inside.
Like the seed which turns to timber, reborn, I am now a member
of your family, which Hell on earth can't hide

Lord, thank you for my friends and my family which tends
to me, Your child, while I am passing through.
On you, my strength depends for you've forgiven all my sins
Hold me fast and close while I cling to you.

Refrain

Carry on, carry on and one day very soon
my yearning heart shall beat as one with Yours.
Then You shall banish all my fears,
in that land that knows no tears,
as you lead me through the doors
to that mansion which holds for each a room.

Phil. 4:7 "And the peace of God, which transcends all understanding,
will guard your hearts and your minds in Christ Jesus"

Carry on, Carry on

Sherlie was my wife's best friend. She was a handsome and charming woman, who was a follower of Jesus. She contracted cancer at a very young age. Her strength and faith right up until the end was an inspiration for her two young sons and for her friends. She is missed by all that knew her.

71

The Keepers

How brave our Pilgrim fathers who hungered for your word,

who carved freedom from this rock, and would not be deterred.

An accident, my birth in this nation, blessing mine

A land foreordained by God to be a cornucopia divine.

Native land of countless blessings, its children born, we grew

as the providential of this world, a truth we scarcely knew.

Then, grown one day we stood. You unveiled lands beyond our pearl.

We gazed on brothers starving in an uncompassionate world.

You exposed man's pain and misery, to awaken a nation's measure.

Old Glory's your gift for sharing, not ours to dissipate in pleasure.

Your graces urge our hearts to share abundance with the rest.

For you have christened us the keepers of America the Blest.

1 John 3:1 "If anyone has material possessions and sees his brother in need but has no pity on him, how can the love of God be in him?"

The Keepers

Does God bless a nation? I think so.
America is the only country founded
on the right to worship God and Christ
without government interference.
True, other beliefs now have the same
worship privileges in this country as do
Christians, but they were not the
founding faith of the
"In God we Trust" that we know.

The Annoyance

The commuters, like a swarm of locusts,
descend into the bowels of the earth below London Town.
Far beneath the city streets,
the tube stops and the crowd
squeezes through its blinking doors,
to herald another day's escape from the
frenetic grasp of finance and business.

All scamper for a seat in the overcrowded train.
The young father and his two toddler children
are the last to enter.
The train chortles up its engine
to meet its mindless schedule.
Holding his two young sandy haired charges,
a boy and a girl, by the hand,
he locates one vacant seat and drops himself wearily into it.

He enfolds the two small children close to him,
fettered by his encircling arms.
In earnest rebellion,
they squirm from his grasp and land on the floor at his feet.
The small boy reaches and yanks his sister's braids.
With a squeal, she is quick to respond in kind.
They tussle, giggle and shriek at each other,
to the dismay of the other passengers.
The father seems oblivious to the commotion as he gazes at a
photograph in his hand.

Increasingly, the passengers find the boisterous
behavior of the juveniles
an unwarranted intrusion in the crowded confines
of the speeding metal cocoon.
Irritated, they dispatch pointed glances towards
the non responsive father.
But, he ignores the haruumphs and barbs.
Occasionally, he will pat the head of one of the
squirming querulous siblings.

Finally, the young executive sitting next to him,
dressed in the rigour London black,
no longer can contain his annoyance.
He turns to the father and utters
sternly to him, speaking for all.
"Say there, my man, perhaps you can have the
wee ones behave a bit more properly"

As if awakened from a trance,
the engrossed father sharply raises his eyes
from the photograph of the young woman
which he slips it into the pocket of his jacket.
He peers down at his children.
Now, acutely aware that his children
are disturbing the others,
he flushes and quickly pulls the toddlers to him and hugs
them, shooing them to quieten.

Pensively He drops his eyes,
then quietly whispers to his traveling companion.
"I apologize for their behavior.
They are confused and distraught as am I.
We just paid the last visit to their Mum at the hospital,
where she slipped away while holding their hands.
I will keep them close to me 'till the stop.
Sorry."

"...heartache crushes the spirit." Proverbs:15:13

The Annoyance

*How many times on the the street or in a
personal encounter do we find ourselves
concluding that behavior of another person is
anti-social or abnormal. Maybe we just haven't
walked a "mile in their shoes". A tragedy can
transform the behavior of the staunchest
Christian and can temporarily "crush their spirit".
So, perhaps we should attempt to not draw
conclusions based upon appearances. I find
when I do that, more often than not,
I am mistaken.*

*T*he *Whisper*

On bended knees once more, my Lord
I promise all
I promise all.

For yet once more, I breach my word.
Again I fall
Again I fall.

How many times, my faith does lack?
Forgive me Lord
Forgive me Lord.

How many times you take me back?
With love restored
With love restored.

My guilt so great. Is lost the race?
I'm bowed with shame
I'm bowed with shame.

Then, a whisper of your grace.
"My blood did clean
My blood did clean."

Matt 26:28 "This is my blood of the covenant,
which is poured out for many for the forgiveness of sins."

Mother

Mother's Day

She rocked and waited in the small retirement home apartment.
Today her sons would come to take her to lunch and make a big deal over her.
She thought back over her eighty one years.
Some memories were bright as day.
Others were clouding a little.

She smiled as she remembered the strong young Carolina farm girl,
helping Daddy with the tobacco crop.
Hated those green tobacco worms, Ugh.
And trying to wash off that tobacco juice from my hands with lye soap...
Imagine girls these days putting lye soap on their skin. That'd be a hoot.
Not a very popular calling these days, growing tobacco, she mused.
Nevertheless, in the 30's that little tobacco money kept soul and family together.
Even let us kids have a little hard candy on Sundays from Rob's old country store.

Huh! Never thought I'd wind up in here, back in those days, she uttered to herself.
In fact, I didn't think of much at all except how to escape from that farm.
A hard life for a girl...
Of course, there were those few times horsing around
in the hayloft with that blond headed boy from down the road.
Now, what was his name? Darn.
Oh, well it flew out and it'll fly back.

And my husband...
Wasn't he something, when I first saw him?
Big brown eyes and that soft smile with those flashing white teeth...
Drove up in the front yard in that shiny black model T
and asked Daddy if he could take me for a ride.

Well, it's been some ride,
Fifty six years with the best, kindest man a woman could hope for.
God, I miss him so. Never thought about losing him.
Never thought I'd have to leave my home either.
Bodies and minds just get plumb tuckered out.
Guess I wasn't much for seeing the future, maybe I didn't want to.

Don't want to think sad thoughts now.
Don't want to be all teared up when the boys get here.
Always tried to be strong around my boys.
What was it the Bible called our kids, the "jewels of our old age"?
Well, they're good boys, but they weren't always jewels.
Sometimes just hardheaded little rocks, she grinned to herself.
God has given me a good life and and loving family.
As for the rest, well, we just have to play the cards we're dealt.

Must be them at the door.
"Happy Mothers Day!"
"Come in boys, Still got the same women huh? Set down girls."
(Hugs all around)
She laughed, "Did you boys bring me some nice presents?
You better had. Hope they're expensive. I deserve them."

"A cheerful heart is good medicine." Proverbs 17:22

Mother's Day

The seasons of life are relentless in their passage through our lives.
Everything is in a lockstep. Our children, as they grow older,
observe us as we grow older, as we observe our beloved parents grow older.
And so on it goes...

My mother, with generally a good spirit, takes life as it comes.
When she was the young mother of my brothers and me, she made
sure that we were off to church on Sundays. She was a great encourager
to her children, letting us know that we could always count on her support.
Her sense of humor endeared her to everyone and has stayed with
her through some hard situations. We were blessed by her devotion to us.

After writing Mother's Day, I had to explain to Mom that
"the blond haired boy in the hayloft" was just my exercise of poetic license.
She didn't buy it.

A *Yuletide Millennium*

"Behold, glad tidings of greatest joy."
Twain thousand years ago a boy,
born heir of heaven, the soul of man,
God's offer of love
with one demand.

Dare we accept? If so we must
submit our heart! Behold the cross
which Jesus bore in pain and shame
that gave us the right
to call his name.

For two thousand years ago today
His courage cleansed our sins away.
And if two thousand comes no more
He'll embrace us
on that distant shore.

Yes, Christmas joy! Savior divine!
My mind recalls, swept back in time,
in misery's grasp, I cried your name.
Into my sinner's heart,
you came.

Such arduous love I never knew
'til that wondrous day You led me through
heaven's portal, for You're the key.
Happy Birthday, Lord
from a grateful me.

A Yuletide Millennium

Truly an old, old story, but one which in the second millenium still alters the life of man, just as it was promised from the beginning.

Celebration

Death has lost its sting.

We are His children.
We are the forgiven.

His spirit within empowers us.
His love surrounds and protects us.
His mansions await us.

Once blind, now we see.

We must tell the world
of the gift that awaits all who confess
that Jesus Christ is Lord.

Glory to His name!

Rejoice in our fortune!

Celebrate!

*John 20:21   "Again Jesus said, 'Peace be with you!
As the Father has sent me, I am sending you.' "*

Tempus Fugit

The doctor stroked his greying beard.

The patient hung on every word.

"I'm afraid the news is bad.

Only 'ten' are left. I know 'tis sad."

The patient paled, then he gasped

"Doctor, doctor, I pray ask

Months or weeks? How much time?

Slowly sighed the doctor, "Nine"

*"So you must also be ready, because the Son of Man will come
at an hour when you do not expect him." Matt. 24:44*

Tempus Fugit

*The collection of poems ends with this whimsical incident which
illustrates the often unexpected encounter with our own mortality.
Sometimes prayer and a sense of humor are our greatest assets in
sorting out the unexpected bumps on this mortal road which we travel.*

Items of Interest to the Reader on Web Site
pandapublications.com

Fund Raising ideas for organizations.

Organizations such as churches and religious associations
may wish to explore fund raising opportunities available
with the sales of this book, Miracle in a Small Mountain
Town, by Allen Autry together with the sales of
James F. William's prints. Bulk sales prices of this book
and prints of Mr. Williams are available on the web site
together with fund raising ideas using the books and prints.

Signed prints of James F. Williams together with a copy of
this book are great sellers at fund raising auctions.

Gift Ideas: *This book and individual James F. Williams prints*

This book together with a print from the book makes wonderful gifts for friends, employees or volunteers.

The reader of this book may wish to purchase one or more
of the illustrations by James F. Williams which are in this
book. These illustrations are available as beautiful signed
limited editions prints for as long as they may last.
Unsigned prints at reasonable prices are also available. In
addition, other works of Mr. Williams are available at the
web site.

Abe's Prayer   *Mission Bay*

Nest for The Killing Bird   *Forgiven*

Village in the Valley

Publishing Credits

Following are the initial publication dates and periodicals of some of the works within this book

"Lord, did you sob with shoulders shaking" The War Cry, national magazine of The Salvation Army, April (Easter issue) 2000

"A Nest for the Killing Bird" The Bread Of Life, January, 2000

"Holy Spirit, Tender Teacher" The Walnut Pulpit, January 2000

"The Redefinement of Love" The Bread of Life, February, 2000